P9-DGE-792

This edition published in 1999 by
CHARTWELL BOOKS, INC.
A division of BOOK SALES, INC
114 Northfield Avenue,
Edison, New Jersey 08837

Produced by
PRC Publishing Ltd,
Kiln House, 210 New Kings Road, London SW6 4NZ

© 1999 PRC Publishing Ltd.

All rights reserved. No part of this publication may
be reproduced, stored in a retrieval system, or transmitted
in any form or by any means, electronic, mechanical,
photocopying, recording, or otherwise, without the
prior written permission of the Publisher and copyright
holders.

ISBN 0 78581 057 9

Printed and bound in Hong Kong

Contents

Introduction

AN EXCELLENT CHINA DRINK

A Chinese tea drinker by the name of Lin Yutang wrote in the 1930s, "The proper enjoyment of tea can only be developed in an atmosphere of leisure, friendship, and sociability, for it is only in the company of those gifted with a sense of comradeship, extremely select in the matter of forming friends and endowed with a natural love of the leisurely life that the full enjoyment of tea becomes possible. Take away the element of sociability and these things have no meaning."

Of all tea's attributes, this element of sociability is probably the strongest, and for all nations around the world who today drink tea, although they may brew, serve, and consume it in different ways, the beverage symbolizes communication, shared moments, sympathy, harmony, and friendship.

The tea story started in China round about the year 2750 BC when the tea plant was found to have a number of medicinal properties. Legend says that an Emperor by the name of Shen Nung was sitting one day in the shade of a wild tea tree, boiling some drinking water, when a breeze blew a few leaves from the tree into the pot and gave the water a flavor that he found delicious. It is said that he experimented further, found it to have medicinal properties as well as a pleasing flavor, and subsequently urged the Chinese people to cultivate the plant for the benefit of the entire nation.

It is actually unlikely that anyone by the name of Shen Nung ever really lived, and it is far more probable that farming tribes in different parts of China gradually discovered the advantages of drinking the herb. But over the centuries, Shen Nung has become the legendary Father of Tea.

introduction

Above: The Brinchang Sungei Palas (Boh) tea plantation in the Pahang Cameron Highlands, Malaysia.

tea

In the early days of tea drinking in China, the green leaves were picked from wild trees and boiled in water to give what was almost certainly a rather bitter brew. Over the centuries, the leaves were chewed, brewed, and stewed — used first as a medicine and later as a pleasurable infusion. By the 4th and 5th centuries AD, tea plantations were established and the plucked leaves were either steamed to remove their bitter taste or dried and pounded, then compressed into cakes. To make an infusion, the cakes were broken into pieces and boiled in water. During the Song Dynasty (AD 960-1279), the leaves were powdered and whisked into boiling water to make a frothy green liquid, then during the Ming Dynasty (AD 1368-1644), the fashion returned for steamed and dried loose leaves. This style of green tea did not keep or travel well and as markets began to expand outside China, Chinese merchants, in order to protect their profits, started to roast the leaves to stop them from rotting. They discovered that if the leaves were spread out in the air and left to oxidize until they turned a reddish-coppery color and were then baked or pan-fried, the black tea that resulted was less likely to deteriorate. This black tea (or red, as the Chinese call it) was manufactured mainly for export and the Chinese continued to drink, and today still drink the infusion of green leaves.

In modern Chinese homes, tea is always served to guests as a sign of welcome and hospitality, and in restaurants, a pot of tea is always the first and the last thing to be brought to the table. On trains, every carriage has a boiler to provide hot water for tea brewing and each compartment has a thermos that is filled and refilled from the boiler throughout the journey. Travelers carry cups or jars, or sometimes covered mugs are supplied by the railway, and conductors sell packs of tea for a few fen. At work, every factory and office has a boiler, and mugs or cups of tea are brewed constantly throughout the working day. Tea houses, which fell from grace during the Cultural Revolution because they were seen as hotbeds of political intrigue and dissent, are now very much back in fashion and appeal to all types and ages. They often serve a large range of different teas which are brewed in glasses, covered mugs or little Chinese teapots and bowls.

Above: Chinese tea caddy.

Below: Illustration from the lid of a Japanese tea chest.

Bottom: A tea shop in China, 1919.

JAPANESE "TEAISM"

From China, the love of tea spread to Japan with Buddhist monks who traveled to and from China for their religious studies. The fact that tea's stimulating properties helped monks to stay awake during meditation and periods of prayer led to its growing importance in Japanese life. The first tea is thought to have been planted in Japan in the 8th century AD, but large-scale commercial cultivation did not start until the 12th century.

Although the custom of whipping powdered green tea into boiling water disappeared from Chinese life, the Japanese developed this method of brewing into a Zen Buddhist ceremony, *Chanoyu*, which still holds a very important place in modern Japanese society.

The Japanese philosophy teaches that "tea is more than an idealization of the form of drinking; it is a religion of the art of life." It takes many years of dedicated study and practice to learn how to perform the elaborate tea ceremony, for every aspect of the event has significance — the actual size and design of the tea house, the flowers and wall decorations, the utensils used, the tea that is served, the movements used during the preparation, the bowls for drinking, the foods that accompany the tea, the way in which the tea is handed to guests, the kimono worn by the hostess, etc.

Today, most Japanese drink green tea, but there has been a noticeable trend over the past few years to turn more to the European style of black tea drinking, with loose leaves or tea bags brewed in a teapot and served with or without milk in cups and saucers. A fondness for British 'afternoon tea' foods has also grown and it is now possible to buy clotted cream, a very British product that until 1997 was not available in Japan, and scones which are deliciously like the British original. Most large Japanese cities now have a number of British style tearooms that serve a variety of green and black teas and a range of typical afternoon tea foods such as sandwiches, scones, and cakes.

Above: The implements used in the Japanese tea ceremony.

Below: The ceremony itself is highly elaborate.

tea

TEATIME IN EUROPE

It was the Portuguese and the Dutch who were the first to import tea to Europe on a regular basis. At the beginning of the 17th century Japanese and Chinese green tea was brought from Java and gradually, awareness of the new commodity grew in Germany, France, and other parts of Europe.

Russia's first experience of tea resulted from a visit in 1618 by a Chinese ambassador to the Russian Czar, although regular trade was not established until 1689. The signing of a new treaty led to camel caravans of tea trekking from Peking across the Gobi Desert to the border with Russia where the tea was traded for furs from Moscow. When the Trans-Siberian Railway opened in 1903, imports of tea no longer traveled by camel but arrived in Moscow by train.

The British seem to have taken very little notice of tea until the end of the 1650s when a London merchant by the name of Thomas Garraway recognized its potential and sold it in leaf and liquid form in his coffee house in Exchange Alley in the city of London. He advertized it as a tonic or medicinal cure for almost any ailment, including stomach disorders, headaches, skin problems, infections, breathing difficulties, colds, influenza, loss of memory, and disturbed sleep.

The marriage of Charles II in 1662 to Catherine of Braganza, a Portuguese princess, certainly played a part in spreading the word about tea, for Catharine was an avid tea drinker long before her arrival in Britain and brought a small casket of leaves with her as part of her dowry. When she started serving it to her friends at court it became the fashionable drink of the time. Over the next 100 years or so, it gradually replaced ale as the everyday beverage and, despite high prices, became Britain's most popular brew. It was drunk at all times of the day but was thought of as particularly beneficial as an after-dinner digestif that helped to settle the stomach after the heavy food that made up the British diet of those days. It was customary for ladies to withdraw to a different room after the main evening meal to gossip over a cup of green or black tea.

Outside the home, tea was initially served in the "coffee houses" that had become popular in the 1650s, and later, when these establishments

Top: The Cutty Sark was the most famous of the many tea clippers that transported tea around the globe.

Above: Workers on the busy London dockside unload the tea.

became too bawdy and disreputable for respectable people, it was in the pleasure gardens of London that a very mixed public, including royalty, aristocrats, and ordinary working people, took tea. The reasonably priced entrance ticket to such places as Vauxhall, Marylebone, and Ranelagh in Chelsea, bought tea with bread and butter, musical entertainment, flowered walks, horse riding, boat rides, firework displays, theatrical productions, acrobats, gambling, and dancing. Sadly, suburban expansion brought about the closure of most of the gardens in the first half of the 19th century.

In the early years of the same century, a new pattern of tea drinking developed when Anna, the 7th Duchess of Bedford, took to drinking tea with a little light food in the middle of the afternoon. The story of the invention of afternoon tea tells how she experienced a "sinking feeling" during the long gap between breakfast at 9 a.m. and dinner at 8.30 or 9 p.m., with only a light luncheon to sustain her at midday. A pot of tea served with some bread and butter was the ideal refreshment at four o'clock, and the Duchess quickly started inviting her friends to join her for tea parties in the middle of the afternoon.

During the 19th century, tea drinking became an essential part of British social life — for all social classes and all ages. Tea parties and events were organized for all possible occasions — informal family teas, tennis teas, picnic teas, elegant afternoon teas, "At Home" tea receptions for up to 200 guests, small intimate teas, wedding teas, children's teas in the nursery, country house teas on the lawn, high teas with robust filling savories such as cheese on toast, meat pies, fish dishes, and salads as well as cakes and tea breads.

By the end of the century, fashion designers were creating fanciful, romantic, flowing gowns in lace, chiffon, silk, and satin for wealthy ladies to wear at teatime, and housekeeping manuals and cookery books gave clear instructions about teatime invitations, etiquette, methods of brewing and serving, table wares, the role of the servant, dress, menus, and food presentation.

London's first tea shop opened in 1864 when the manageress of the London Bridge branch of the Aerated Bread Company had the

Above: Vauxhall Pleasure Gardens, a popular place for many in the 18th century where tea was taken while the revellers enjoyed the many diversions.

Below: A tea party in India at the height of the British Empire.

idea of using the back room of the bakery as a tearoom. Other companies followed her example and soon there were tearooms all over Britain that attracted all ages and all types and served cheap pots of tea as well as hot and cold, sweet and savory foods, and sometimes employed orchestras and bands to entertain their clientele. When some of the large elegant hotels opened during the Edwardian period from 1901 to 1914, most offered afternoon teas in lounges or palm courts where string quartets, harpists or palm court trios provided genteel background music while wealthy ladies and gentlemen sipped their tea from fine bone china cups and nibbled dainty cucumber and smoked salmon sandwiches.

In 1913, a new dimension was added to teatime when the Tango arrived in a blaze of publicity from Argentina. The first Tango was seen in a London stage production called *The Sunshine Girl* in 1912 and soon everyone wanted to learn the steps to this exotic and risqué Latin dance. Hotels, restaurants, and theaters arranged classes, fashion designers adapted the afternoon tea gown to the demands of the flamboyant steps and kicks, raised hemlines a little, and added satin ribbons to shoes to ensure that the delicate dance slippers stayed on the feet. "Tango Tea Dances" became all the rage across the land, and held a colorful place in society until the 1920s when cocktails became more fashionable and the war brought radical changes to the lifestyle of most social classes.

The increased popularity of the tea bag from the 1950s onwards changed the way in which Britain brewed and drank tea and much of the elegance and ceremony disappeared. Teashops were gradually replaced by fast food restaurants and coffee bars, and tea, although still popular at home, played a rather less important role in public. However, the early 1980s saw a renaissance for tea. New tearooms opened in unlikely places and attracted customers from all walks of life, a few speciality shops appeared in busy high streets and sold a wider variety of quality teas, the media started talking about Britain's favorite beverage, tea dances became popular again in London hotels and provincial dance halls, and foreign tourists to Britain began to show a serious interest in afternoon tea. Tea now features regularly on food and drink radio and television pro-

Above and Below: Tea dances were popular with young and old alike.

grammes, stars in countless newspaper and magazine articles, is a central part of the service offered by most hotels, links into events at museums and art galleries, is a focus for major charity fund raising activities, and attracts new aficionados every day.

Afternoon tea today consists of three elements — neat sandwiches filled with interesting mixtures such as smoked salmon with dill and horseradish, cream cheese with chives and cucumber, smoked ham with whole grain mustard, turkey with cranberry jelly, prawns with a marie rose dressing; warm scones served with preserves and clotted cream; pastries and cakes such as chocolate *mille feuille*, praline flavored eclairs, fruit tartlets, and traditional fruit cakes. A "cream tea" consists of scones served with jams and clotted cream, and "high tea" still includes more filling hot and cold savory treats as well as cakes and desserts.

TEA IN AMERICA

As European groups traveled to the new colonies of North America, they took their tea drinking habits and essential equipment with them and so, even before the British took over New Amsterdam from the Dutch and renamed it New York, tea was an established part of life there.

But problems between Britain and her American colonies developed when the British government attempted to impose heavy import taxes on tea and other commodities to pay for the upkeep of the British army and government officials in America. The unrest that followed led to the Boston Tea Party in 1773, when 340 chests of tea were tipped overboard from ships belonging to the British East India Company by men dressed as native American Indians. When the British government closed Boston harbor and sent in troops to calm the troubles, the long-term result was the War of Independence and the end of America's affection for tea.

Although America is thought of today as a coffee drinking nation, those political disagreements of the 18th century have long since been forgiven and forgotten and America is enjoying a revival of interest in tea: more and more tea shops have opened, a wide variety of speciality shops and mail order companies are offering a carefully chosen range of teas from

Above: The Boston Tea Party in Boston Harbor, 1773. Dressed as Native Americans, a group of Bostonians board a British ship laden with imported tea and throw the full crates into the harbor.

Below: Nearly two centuries later a tea shop in Boston. The giant teapot attatched to the shop's facade spouts steam.

all over the world, and the healthy, calming aspects of tea drinking are appreciated by more and more people.

Because of higher average temperatures than those enjoyed by Britain, many Americans prefer iced tea to hot tea, but the fashion for British style hot black tea served with milk is growing.

TEA AROUND THE WORLD

In India, tea is served and drunk in a number of different ways. Sometimes it is brewed and served in the British style with milk and sugar, or leaves are boiled with milk, water, spices, and sugar. On street corners, railway stations and trains, sweet milky tea is poured from hot kettles into disposable cups or mugs.

In Tibet, green brick tea is broken up and boiled in water then strained into a churn and mixed with goat's or yak's milk, butter, and salt.

In Egypt, tea is brewed strong and served in glasses without milk, and sometimes flavored with sugar or mint leaves. Similarly, in Morocco, black tea is brewed with sugar and mint in a long-spouted pot and is then poured in a thin stream into tall glasses. The Turkish also serve their black tea in curved glasses and offer it on trays to visitors at home or in shops and offices throughout the day.

Iran and Afghanistan drink green tea as a thirst quencher and black tea as a satisfying warming refreshment from little porcelain bowls. In Russia the samovar still holds pride of place in many households. Russians drink both green and black tea, usually from glasses. Traditionally, they take a piece of sugar or a spoonful of jam into their mouths before sipping the tea.

In Africa, where several countries are now very important producers of black tea, strong tea is brewed and served in the same way as in Britain and drunk with milk.

What is Tea?

More than 3,000 different teas are produced in many places around the world and they are all made from one plant — the *Camellia sinensis*. This tea plant has two subspecies, the *Camellia sinensis sinensis* (a native bush of China which can withstand cold climates), and *Camellia sinensis assamica* (a tree which

Above: A traditional Cornish cream tea.

Left: Serving tea from a Russian samovar.

flourishes in tropical locations). It is indigenous to China, Tibet, and northern India but today is grown in many countries that lie close to the equatorial belt around the globe — in Japan, China, Taiwan, Vietnam, Indonesia, Africa, India, Nepal, Bangladesh, Sri Lanka, South America, Malaysia, Australia, Papua New Guinea, and others.

The plant is an evergreen that produces small white blossoms with tiny yellow stamens and dark shiny leaves that vary in size depending on the sub-species and variant of the plant. For commercial growing, new plants are grown from the seeds inside the little fruits that develop from each flower, or from leaf cuttings. These baby plants are nurtured in the tea nursery until they are two years old. They are then pruned back and allowed to grow again but are pruned regularly to keep them at waist height. Plucking can start when the new bush is between three and five years old, depending on the climatic conditions and the altitude.

The way in which just one plant can produce teas that are so different from each other is very similar to the way in which grapes can produce so many different types of wine. The plant grows differently and the leaves give a different taste depending on a number of variable factors — the geographical location, the height of the mountains on whose slopes the tea grows, the soil and mineral contents, the seasons, the climate, the method of cultivation, the way in which the leaves are picked, the time of year when the leaves are harvested, the manufacturing process, and what happens to the leaves after manufacture — the sorting, blending, packing, transportation, and storage.

The tea plant likes warm temperatures, humidity, and plenty of rainfall. The finest teas grow at elevations of more than 3,000ft (915m) where cool temperatures in the early morning and evening slow the rate at which new shoots are pushed out, where the intense heat during the day encourages the development of flavor in the leaves, and where the clouds that swirl around mountain peaks feed the plant with the moisture that they love.

If allowed to grow freely, the tea bush or tree will grow to heights of 15-60ft (4.5-18m), but for commercial production, the plants are pruned and plucked to waist height to make for easy plucking.

Above: A tea picker in Sri Lanka.

Below: A tea field in Makinohara, Japan.

The new growth of the tea bush is called the "flush" and depending on the climate, the plant may go on flushing all year, as in Africa and Indonesia. If the region is more seasonal, this may mean that the plant stops growing during the colder winter and only flushes during the warmer months.

In order to produce good quality tea, the general rule is that a picker plucks a bud and the first two young leaves from the top of each new shoot. This is usually done by hand — the best method for ensuring that only the most suitable tender leaves are gathered — but in certain tea producing areas, a labor shortage or expensive labor rates mean that the tea is harvested by machines which cut off more twigs and older leaves and the resulting tea is of a poorer quality.

The tea pickers carry the picked leaves in baskets or bags on their backs and at the end of each picking period, the leaves are transported back to the factory which is usually on or near the plantation. Pickers are paid by the weight of leaf they gather each day.

DIFFERENT TYPES OF TEA

Tea is generally categorized into six different types — white, green, oolong, black, flavored, and compressed. White teas are made by drying the buds of a variant of the tea plant that grows high up on Chinese mountains. Tiny silver hairs that cover the buds give the tea a white appearance. Compressed teas are green or black teas that have been packed tightly into little round flat or nest-like cakes or into slab-shaped bricks. Both white and compressed teas are rarely found outside China.

It was thought at one time that green teas and black teas came from completely different plants, but it is only the manufacturing process that produces the different kinds.

Green Tea

To make green tea, the plucked leaves are laid out in the sun or in the warm air of the factory and are allowed to wither until they are slightly limp and soft. They are then heat-treated to destroy any enzymes that would react with the oxygen in the air and cause the leaf to rot. Green teas are therefore generally known as unfermented or unoxidized teas. Heat is applied either by pan-frying in a large wok, as

Top: Chinese tea has been compressed into a block.

Above: Within the "string" are balls of tea while outside are small "nests."

in China, or by steaming, as in Japan. This is followed by rolling on heated trays — a process that is sometimes done by machine and sometimes by hand; the way in which the leaves are rolled affects the final appearance of the tea. For example, Gunpowder tea is rolled into little round pellets that look a little like lead shot — hence the name — while other green teas are twisted or flat.

After rolling, the leaves are fired in large dryers to remove more of their water content. Some green teas are repeatedly rolled and dried — individual producers having developed their own methods of manufacturing over the centuries to create each tea's particular characteristics.

Green tea leaves give a straw colored or pale greenish-yellow or brownish-yellow liquor and generally have a somewhat astringent or pungent flavor. They are produced mainly in China, Japan, and Taiwan, but small amounts are also manufactured in India and Sri Lanka.

Oolong Tea

Oolong tea is often called semi-fermented or semi-oxidized tea and is principally produced in the Fujian province of China, and in Taiwan. Other countries such as Sri Lanka and India produce only very small amounts of oolong.

The time of picking is crucial for the production of quality oolongs. The leaves must be neither too young nor too mature and as soon as they have been picked, they are wilted for four or five hours in direct sunlight or in warm air inside the factory to remove some of the water content. They are then shaken in bamboo baskets to bruise and gently break the edges of the leaf to allow the natural juices to react with oxygen in the air. The leaves are then alternately spread out and left to oxidize in warm air and are shaken or rolled, sometimes in baskets and sometimes inside cloth bags that are rolled by hand or in a machine. The color of the leaf gradually changes and the center of the leaf remains a yellowy green while the edges, where the enzymes have oxidized, become reddy-brown. The leaves start to give off a smell similar to orchids or peaches. The longer the period of oxidation, the darker in color the leaves will become.

The oxidation, or fermentation, is stopped by firing the leaves at high temperatures either in pans or ovens.

Top: Gunpowder tea.

Center: Oolong from Taiwan.

Bottom: Formosa Pouchong from Taiwan — similar to oolong but oxidized for a shorter time.

Oolong teas give a light golden-red liquor with a gentle, sometimes peachy, aroma and a light delicate flavor.

Black Tea

The Chinese refer to this as red tea because of the color of the liquor it produces. Manufacturing processes vary from country to country, but there are two basic methods — "orthodox" and CTC (cut, tear, and curl). All black teas, both orthodox and CTC, go through four basic stages — withering, rolling, oxidation, and firing.

For the production of orthodox teas, once the leaves have been plucked, they are laid out in warm air and allowed to wither for between 18 and 24 hours to remove a certain proportion of their water content and to make them soft and limp enough to roll without splitting the surface. They are then rolled in a machine that twists and breaks the leaves to release the natural chemicals that later react with oxygen in the air and give the final black tea its characteristic smell and taste. After rolling, the leaves are broken up and spread out in cool air for 3½-4½ hours to oxidize. The chemical reaction that takes place changes the color of the leaves from green to a coppery red color. They are constantly checked and the changing appearance and smell are a guide as to when they are ready for the next stage of firing. As the oxidation period goes on longer for black teas than for oolongs, the appearance of the final product is much blacker.

To stop the oxidation, the leaves are fired, either in large pans or in oven-like dryers that remove all but the last 3% of the water in the leaf. The tea turns black and develops its characteristic slightly burnt smell and flavor.

The CTC process of manufacture produces tiny particles of leaf that brew quickly and are therefore ideal for use in tea bags. Instead of being gently rolled after withering, they are put through a machine that chops them into tiny pieces. The oxidation and firing of the tea is exactly the same as for orthodox teas.

The CTC method of manufacture was developed in the 1950s when tea bags became more and more popular and demanded pieces of leaf that took only two or three minutes to brew. The general rule is that the smaller the pieces of black leaf, the quicker the tea brews. The larger pieces of orthodox teas require four or

Top: Keemun — black tea from China.

Center: Indonesian black CTC tea.

Bottom: Lapsang souchong — Chinese smoky black tea.

five minutes to release their full flavor and color into the boiling water.

Black teas are produced in China, Taiwan, India, Bangladesh, Sri Lanka, Africa, South America, Cameroon, CIS, Iran, Malaysia, Nepal, Turkey, Vietnam, Australia, Papua New Guinea, and America.

Flavored Teas

Ever since the Chinese started manufacturing tea, they have added different flavorings either to the processed dry leaf or to the brew. There was a time when onions, cloves, salt, and sweet herbs were added, but, more commonly, fruits and flowers have been used to perfume or flavor the tea — lychee, bergamot (a citrus fruit also known as the Chinese orange), jasmine, rose, gardenia, honeysuckle, orchid, and magnolia being the most popular. The base for a scented or flavored tea can be green, oolong or black leaf, or a blend of different types. The additional flavorings are mixed with the dry leaf at the end of the basic manufacturing process. The leaf tea is placed into a large bin or mixing machine, the flavoring is added slowly in the form of dry granules or liquid as the tea is continuously tumbled. Alternatively, the tea is spread out on a flat surface and the flavoring is sprayed on. After all the leaves have been exposed to the flavor, either in a mixer or laid out flat, they are spread out on a clean dry surface to dry for about 10-20 minutes, then stored in a covered container for the flavor to develop fully before packaging takes place.

Today's fashion for flavored teas has led the major blending companies to create a very wide range to add to the existing Chinese varieties. The ingredients used are either natural flavors distilled or extracted from flowers, fruits, herbs or spices, or nature identical or artificial flavors, the production of which is tightly controlled by government regulations. Among the most popular flavored teas are Earl Grey (the world's best known speciality tea flavored with bergamot), strawberry, passion fruit, forest fruits, vanilla, blackcurrant, mango, and cinnamon.

HERBAL AND FRUIT INFUSIONS

There is a certain confusion about the difference between teas, flavored teas and other infusions. Flavored teas are made with leaves of

Top: Rose pouchong from China — black tea flavored
with rose petals.

Center: Earl Grey.

Bottom: Genmoucha: Japanese green tea flavored with
toasted rice and popped corn.

the tea plant *Camellia sinensis* which have fruits, flowers, spices, and herbs added. Infusions (also called *tisanes*) are made from other plants and herbs such as camomile, mint, fennel, summer fruits, etc, and do not contain any part of *Camellia sinensis*. Most herbal, fruit, and flower infusions or *tisanes* offer particular benefits and characteristics but they are not officially "teas."

SORTING AND GRADING TEAS

At the end of the manufacturing process, the leaf particles are sorted into different sizes or "grades," As they come out of the dryers, they pass over a system of moving sifter belts with small holes of different sizes through which the particles of tea are shaken to separate the pieces into different grades. In some factories, the tea is still sorted by hand.

The different sized pieces are given names that differentiate between leaf grades — the larger pieces, and the "brokens" as well as the smaller particles. Grading also takes into account the appearance of the tea. For example, some black teas contain lots of little "tips" that are golden or silvery in color. These are the very tips of the buds and leaves that do not darken during manufacture and show that the new leaves were picked carefully by hand and then carefully withered and rolled before oxidation.

Grading is a crucial part of the final processing because when tea is brewed, the different sized pieces infuse their color, strength, and flavor into the boiling water at different speeds — the smaller the pieces of leaf, the quicker the infusion develops. For a pot of tea, or a tea bag to give a quality brew, the pieces of leaf need to be of a standard size. And when different teas are blended together to create, for example, a Breakfast Blend or a Four o'Clock Blend, each packet must contain pieces that are the same size. If not, the smaller pieces will sink to the bottom and the balance of the blend will be lost.

GRADING TERMINOLOGY

Different producing countries may use the following terms differently as there is no absolutely universal system of grading. Chinese teas are often given a name from the area in which they

Three herbal infusions from Sussex Teas.
Top: Apple Viennese
Center: Berry fruit cocktail.
Bottom: Peach and apple.

Below: Grading on the Ambootia™ estate.

are produced, or from the method of manufacture, or from a legend that surrounds the particular tea, and they may then be further graded according to quality, seasonal pickings, etc.

The following terms are generally only used for black teas. Green teas are graded differently depending on which part of the new shoot is used and whether the bud is open or still wrapped by the new leaves.

Flowery Orange Pekoe (FOP)
Made from the bud and first new leaf of each shoot; fine tender young leaves with a good proportion of tip. Pekoe derives from the Chinese word for the tiny hairs or down on the underside of the young leaf. A Pekoe grade is virtually a whole leaf.

Golden Flowery Orange Pekoe (GFOP)
FOP with golden tips.

Tippy Golden Flowery Orange Pekoe (TGFOP)
FOP with a large amount of golden tips.

Finest Tippy Golden Flowery Pekoe (FTGFOP)
Very high quality FOP.

Orange Pekoe (OP)
Long pointed leaves plucked as the new leaf bud is just opening.

Pekoe (P)
Shorter, less high quality than OP.

Flowery Pekoe (FP)
Leaves that are rolled into little balls.

Pekoe Souchong (PS)
Shorter, rougher pieces of leaf.

Souchong (S)
Large leaves that have been rolled to give coarse pieces with a ragged appearance.

Broken Orange Pekoe (BOP)
Broken or smaller leaf.

Fannings (F)
Very small broken particles of leaf, made by the orthodox or CTC process. CTC fannings are more granular.

Top: Flowery broken orange pekoe.

Center: Whole leaf grade from China.

Bottom: Flowery pekoe.

Dust (D)
The very smallest particles.

Pekoe Fannings/Pekoe Dust
Chunkier, grainy particles resulting from CTC manufacture.

Fannings and Dusts are mostly used in blends for tea bags because they brew very quickly and give a good color.

SINGLE SOURCE TEAS AND BLENDS

Due to variations in weather patterns and all the other variables that play a part in the final flavor and quality of teas from different regions around the world, the teas produced by each plantation or smallholder are different each season or each year. Some tea connoisseurs enjoy these differences in the same way that wine connoisseurs enjoy the differences in the flavor of wines from different vineyards and wine-producing regions. They look forward to tasting and assessing the teas manufactured after each plucking or each season. This kind of speciality tea is marketed with the name of the particular tea garden or estate clearly marked on the packet or caddy.

Other tea drinkers prefer to know that each time they open their favorite packet of tea, it will taste the same. In order to fill the packet on the supermarket or tea retailer's shelves with tea that will satisfy this preference, each company of packers and blenders employs a team of tea tasters who decide which mixture of teas from around the world is needed to create that standard flavor and quality.

Each day, these skilled tasters brew and taste hundreds of tea samples that have been sent from plantations in all the major producing countries. Once they have decided which teas are most suitable, they create a recipe for a specific blend that may include up to 35 different teas from different countries or different regions of the same country. The selected teas are then tumbled together in a large drum to ensure an even distribution of leaf before the tea is packaged into tea bags, packets or caddies of loose leaf tea.

Above: A single source tea from the Thotulagala estate in Ceylon.

Below: The Ambootia™ estate is famed as a single source supplier of organic teas.

LOOSE LEAF TEA OR TEA BAGS

It is true that loose leaf tea will almost always give a better cup of tea than tea bags. Tea bags were invented in the US in 1908 when a tea merchant by the name of John Sullivan decided to send samples of tea to his customers in small silk bags. The idea was that they should tip the leaves into their tea pot in the normal way but his intentions were misinterpreted and the little bag was put directly into the pot so that the leaves infused through the tiny holes in the fabric. Apparently his customers liked the fact that the tea was measured out into suitable portions and that there was no leaf deposit to dispose of from the teapot after brewing. The invention led to a demand for more and more tea bags and by the 1950s, Sullivan's silk had been replaced first by gauze and then by paper. By 1960, tea bags accounted for 5% of tea sales in the UK. By 1965, the use of bags had increased to 7%, and by 1993, tea bags were being used for 85% of tea brewed in Britain. In the US, between 65% and 70% of tea consumed is brewed using tea bags.

The majority of tea that goes into tea bags is made by the CTC method of manufacture and most tea experts agree that although bags give a quick colory brew, tea made in this way lacks the fine and subtle characteristics of larger leaf, orthodox teas. Many people think that brewing tea with tea bags is easier and much less messy than with loose leaf tea, but by using an infuser that can be lifted out of tea pots, cups or mugs, good quality loose leaf tea can be brewed quickly, easily, and without any fuss to give a much more interesting and satisfying beverage. This method of brewing also allows tea drinkers to try some of the world's unusual teas that are not generally available in tea bags.

HOW TO BREW THE PERFECT CUP OF TEA

Different types of tea need different water temperatures and different infusion times, but there are a few golden rules for the brewing of perfect tea. These rules apply for the brewing of black or oolong teas, either in tea bags or in the form of loose leaves. Green tea should always be made with water that has boiled and been allowed to cool for a few minutes to a temperature of between 158°F and 194°F (70°C and 90°C).

Above: Tea bags are typically filled with fannings or dust grounds.

Bottom: The perfect brew.

Fill the kettle or pot with freshly drawn cold water (it must contain oxygen in order to bring out the full flavor of tea).

When the water is nearly boiling, pour a little into the teapot, swill round, and tip away, leaving a hot, clean, empty teapot.

Measure the tea carefully into the pot, allowing one rounded teaspoon 0.1oz (2.5g) or one teabag for each cup required (this will vary according to the type of tea used and personal preference of strength etc).

Take the teapot to the boiling kettle or pot of water and, as the water is coming to a rolling boil, pour it directly onto the leaves or bags.

Replace the lid of the teapot and leave to infuse for the required number of minutes. Recommended brewing times are sometimes given by individual companies on the side of the packet.

BUYING AND STORING TEAS

A good selection of teas is now available from supermarkets, quality department stores, specialist tea retailers, and by mail order (via catalogues and the internet).

Tea keeps better in the larger containers used for storage by tea merchants and mail order companies, so it is best to buy small quantities for home use, store it carefully, and use it as fresh as possible.

It should be possible to buy a few ounces or grams at a time in order to try different types of tea before deciding which to buy in larger quantities. The retailer or merchant should be able to give details and advice about the teas, their origins, characteristics, brewing times, etc. Choose a supplier accordingly.

The individual choice of which teas to buy depends on personal taste. For those people who prefer a strong, robust tea, choose Assam and African teas or blends that include teas from these regions. Darjeeling teas are often described as astringent and quite "green" in flavor and are sought by connoisseurs all around the world for their subtle undertones of muscatel grape and raisin flavors, and for those who prefer a flavory but gentler brew, Sri Lanka offers a wide range of teas with a subtle golden liquor. China's black teas are generally lighter than teas from the Indian sub-continent, and for a very light, low caffeine infusion to be drunk without milk, choose a China oolong.

Top: Two different infusion devices which should fit into most teapots.

Above: A typical Japanese tea caddy is excellent for storing tea.

Green teas have a pungency and aromatic quality that is currently appealing to more and more tea drinkers and is accepted as having a gently beneficial effect on the digestion, so is excellent as an after-dinner option.

Store loose tea and tea bags in an airtight tin, box or caddy (not made of glass) so that they are cool, dark, and away from other strong smelling foods such as garlic, spices, etc. Tea absorbs moisture and other flavors very easily, but stored carefully, loose leaf tea will keep well for up to two years. Tea bags tend to dry out much more quickly, so do not leave in the cardboard box they are bought in but transfer immediately to a box or tin with a tight fitting lid.

ORGANIC TEA

The aims of organic tea producers is to grow a crop that is free from chemicals in an environmentally conscious way that does not place human health at risk, uses renewable resources, protects plant and wildlife, replenishes soil fertility and productivity, and minimizes damage to the environment.

This does not mean that non-organic teas contain chemicals (indeed tea is a very clean crop and use of any pesticides and fertilizers is very strictly controlled by European law), but rather that organic growers place an emphasis on care for the environment and the long-term well-being of the planet.

Cultivation under an organic system is complicated and rigidly controlled by the international certification bodies who carry out regular inspections of the plantation, the soil, the processing plants, any vehicles used, and any other equipment involved in the production of the tea.

DECAFFEINATED TEA

For people who enjoy the taste of tea but do not wish to take in any caffeine, decaffeinated teas are now available. Three methods of removing caffeine from teas (after oxidizing and firing the leaves) are used, and researchers are still debating which is best. Carbon dioxide is the most widely used and is thought to be the least harmful. Methylene chloride is the cheapest and most easily removed from the tea after the decaffeination process.

However, the US and Germany ban all

Above: The Ambootia™ estate makes organic tea which is sold to various suppliers around the world.

imports of products using methylene chloride. Ethyl acetate is more difficult to remove from the tea after decaffeination but since small traces occur naturally in tea, some believe this to be the best method.

Decaffeinated tea is not totally free of caffeine — approximately 3% still remains in the leaf after decaffeination.

TEA AND HEALTH

Tea is a natural product which contains no preservatives, no artificial colorings or additives (other than the flavorings in flavored teas), and is virtually calorie free when drunk without milk or sugar.

It contains trace elements (potassium, manganese, folic acid) and vitamins (A, B1, B2) that are needed as part of the body's daily intake.

Tea is thought to aid digestion, help reduce blood cholesterol, protect the teeth against plaque and tooth decay, increase alertness, reduce fatigue, and improve concentration. But the most significant health benefit is the role played by the polyphenols that are found in all teas.

These polyphenols have been identified as antioxidants that help to protect the body against free radicals (produced by our bodies and found in pollution in the air, cigarette smoke and the sun's rays) that provoke ageing and can cause the development of cancer cells. Recent research has found that by drinking regular cups of tea we can help protect our bodies against certain cancers, thrombosis, and stroke.

Tisanes make a refreshing alternative to traditional teas
and have no caffiene content. They can be bought
either loose or in bags.

tea

Assam Second Flush

Newby Teas Ltd
105 St John Street
London EC1M 4AS
UK
Tel: (00 44) (0)171 251 8939
Fax: (00 44) (0)171 251 8928

Trading problems with China at the beginning of the 19th century led the British to look for a suitable location in which to grow their own tea and the plant was discovered growing in the state of Assam in north eastern India. Plantations were established there and the first shipment of eight chests of Assam tea was auctioned in London in 1838. The main tea growing areas are along both sides of the River Brahmaputra in a valley where plenty of rain throughout the year and high temperatures create a heat and humidity that the tea bushes thrive upon.

The first teas of the season are plucked from March to May and these are seldom marketed separately, but the second flush, gathered in June, gives delicious teas that are highly prized by connoisseurs. The new leaves and buds are covered on the underside with lots of tiny white hairs and give the tea its excellent quality.

Toganagoan Estate is one of the largest in the Assam Valley, stretching over an area of 4.6 square miles (1,200 hectares). The first bushes were planted in 1926 and the size of the garden has increased with the success of its teas.

Characteristics: Substantial pieces of black leaf with plenty of golden tips. Gives a fruity bouquet with flowery undertones and a taste that is malty and rounded with a suggestion of raspberry jam.

Brewing hints: Infuse in boiling water for three-four minutes.

Drinking suggestions: An excellent breakfast or all day tea. Good with strong flavored foods. Best drunk with a little milk.

Supplier: Newby Teas is a recently established company with connections to estates in India and dealing with fine quality teas from around the world.

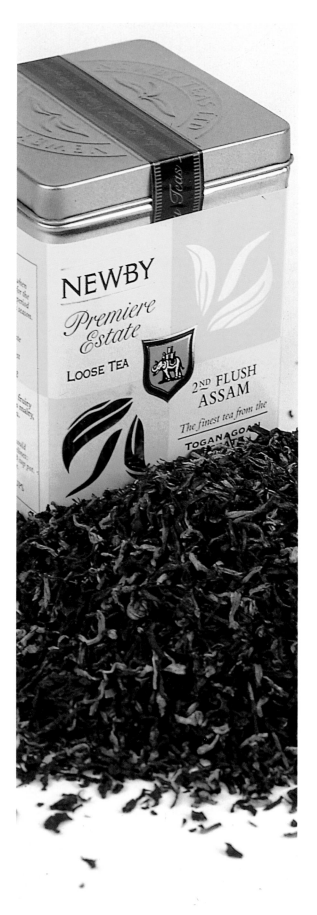

tea

Assam Blend

H. R. Higgins Ltd
79 Duke Street
London W1M 6AS
UK
Tel: (00 44) (0)171 629 3913
Fax: (00 44) (0)171 491 8819

Assam is one of the world's largest tea growing regions and produces more than 450,000 tons of tea a year. During the busiest plucking season, from July to September, each picker gathers approximately 50,000 new new shoots. They work for eight hours a day in very hot and uncomfortably humid conditions and in cases where estates cannot employ enough to pluck the drop, mechanical harvesting machines are sometimes used but do not pick so selectively and therefore give a poorer quality tea.

Assam teas plucked during the earlier part of the growing season are mostly manufactured by the orthodox method whereby the leaves are rolled in a machine after withering and before oxidation. However, the teas that are picked from July to September when rainfall is at its heaviest, have been found to be more suited to CTC (cut, tear, and curl) production whereby the leaves are cut into much smaller pieces and give a tea that brews more quickly. These "rain" teas still have the rich rounded flavor that is so typical of Assams and are often used in breakfast blends along with teas from Africa and Sri Lanka.

Characteristics: Small black pieces of leaf that give a rich red liquor with a malty, full-bodied flavor.

Brewing hints: Brew for two to three minutes in boiling water.

Drinking suggestions: Good for first thing in the morning or for breakfast with fried foods or toast and marmalade.

Supplier: H. R. Higgins, a true family business, and coffee merchants to the Queen, also sells a range of quality teas from the company's Piccadilly premises in London.

Ceylon Nuwara Eliya

Whittard of Chelsea
73 Northcote Road
London SW11 6PJ
UK
Tel: (00 44) (0)171 924 1888
Fax: (00 44) (0)171 924 3085

The highlands of Ceylon where the majority of the tea growing areas are concentrated cover an area of about 4,000 square miles (1 million hectares) of irregular hills and craggy peaks, open valleys and grassy plains, dense forests and deep ravines. Sri Lanka's weather patterns vary from the intense heat of the coastal areas to the temperate climate of the hilly regions where mist and cooler temperatures suit the tea plants and give the leaf its unique bright flavor.

The teas are classified as low grown (sea level-1,800ft/550m), medium grown (1,800-3,500ft/550-1,050m) and high grown (above 3,500ft/1,050m).

The low lying area around the former capital, Kandy, was once the center of the tea growing region and from there roads wind up into the hill country where the finest teas are produced. Nuwara Eliya lies at the foot of the island's highest mountain on a plateau more than 6,000ft (2,100m) up. Since there is no winter and the days are of almost equal length from January to December, the teas can be plucked throughout the year, with the best being manufactured in January and February.

Characteristics: This Nuwara Eliya from Whittard of Chelsea gives a light liquor that has a clean and bright, greenish, crisp flavor.

Brewing hints: Infuse in boiling water for four to five minutes.

Drinking suggestions: Drink with or without milk as an excellent all day tea.

Supplier: Whittard of Chelsea has been selling teas and coffees since 1886 and has more than 100 shops in the UK, in Japan, and other parts of the world.

Whittard offer a range of Ceylon teas, all of which are of
a superb quality.

tea

Ceylon Uva

Robert Wilson's Ceylon Teas
Stonehaven
North Perrott
Crewkerne
Somerset TA18 7SX
UK
Tel/Fax: (00 44) (0)1460 77508

Cinnamon and coffee were once the major crops grown on the beautiful, fertile teardrop-shaped island off the south east of India that today is called Sri Lanka. But in the 1860s, the "coffee rust" blight wiped out almost all the coffee plantations, and experiments with the tea plant were carried out to see if that could provide an alternative source of income. From the 1870s, tea production expanded rapidly as pioneers and planters from England and Scotland gradually developed the industry.

Most of Sri Lanka's tea gardens lie in two areas of the south western inland part of the island at heights ranging from 200ft (60m) to 8,000ft (2,500m) above sea level. The low grown teas have no particularly special qualities but the high growns, from Uva, Dimbula and Nuwara Eliya, give spectacular, rich golden infusions with an intense, fully rounded taste. The teas from each area have their own individual characteristics and the hot dry Cachan winds that blow over the Uva district on the eastern slopes of the central mountains give its teas a concentrated mellow flavor and a wonderful aroma.

St James's Estate produces its best teas in July each year but the unpredictable building and dying of the winds can affect each year's flavor and quality.

Characteristics: Dark brown, fairly large, open leaf with golden tips gives a more colory liquor than some Uvas, with a delicately balanced flavor.

Brewing hints: Brew for four to five minutes in boiling water.

Drinking suggestions: The delicate flavor is best without milk but some people may like to add just a little.

Supplier: Robert Wilson's family connections in Ceylon go back to the 1830s and he now imports a range of quality loose leaf teas from some of Sri Lanka's finest estates.

Robert Wilson's 'Ceylon' Teas

A FAMILY OF PLANTERS & AGENTS
SINCE 1840

CEYLON TEA

China Oolong Tekuanyin

Imperial Tea Court
1411 Powell Street
San Francisco
CA 94133
USA
Tel: (001) 415 788 6080
Fax: (001) 415 788 6079
e.mail: imperial@imperialtea.com

Most of China's oolong teas come from the south eastern province of Fujian which also produces jasmine teas and Lapsang Souchong. Manufacture of oolong teas starts with the withering of freshly gathered leaves in sunlight or by warm air machines. This is followed by several stages of rolling to bruise the edges of the leaves and drying to evaporate most of the water content. In between the various stages, a certain amount of oxidation takes place and this causes the bruised parts of the leaves to turn a coppery color, while the middle stays greeny-brown.

Tekuanyin is a the most famous of Fujian's oolongs and the name means "Tea of the Iron Goddess of Mercy." The explanation comes from the legend that explains how the goddess appeared to a farmer in a dream and instructed him to look in the cave behind her temple. From the single tea shoot that he found there, he cultivated this wonderful tea. The variety of tea plant used to make the tea is today also called Tikuanyin.

The Chinese brew oolong in small pottery teapots and add more hot water several times as the leaves will go on releasing their fragrant flavor.

Characteristics: Dark, crinkly leaves that unfurl to show their pink veins and edges. The infusion has a deep, fragrant flavor.

Brewing hints: Rinse the leaves in boiling water, then brew for five minutes. Add more water for second and third infusions.

Drinking suggestions: Drink without milk at any time of day.

Supplier: Imperial Tea Court, established in 1993, fulfils Roy and Grace Fong's dedication to the art of tea. They specialize in China's rarest teas.

Chun Mee

Mariage Frères
91 rue Alexandre Dumas
75020 Paris
FRANCE
Tel: (00 33) (1)40 09 81 18
Fax: (00 33) (1)40 09 88 15

This famous Chinese green tea is also often called eyebrow tea because of the shape of the pieces of leaf. The way in which the leaves are shaped for different green teas is often complicated and involves several stages. For the production of one particular tea (Lung Ching) 25 steps are described including ten different movements of the hands to shape, stretch, press, and turn the leaf. And as individual farmers and factories have developed their own methods, so the final appearance, aroma, and flavor of the tea are subtly different. Leaves are sometimes shiny, sometimes dull, some are flat and sharp edged, other are twisted or wiry.

Chun Mee leaves are delicately curved like a lady's brows. The pieces are made from little fat buds that are covered with tiny white hairs. Careful temperature control, timing, and very specific movements of the hands are needed to ensure that the shape of the finished tea is exactly right. The tea was originally called Famous Plum because of its plum-like flavor and the fact that it comes from a place whose name translates as Upper Plum Islet.

Characteristics: Tiny brow-shaped leaves that give a clear, golden yellow liquor with a smooth, plummy taste.

Brewing hints: Brew in water that has boiled and been allowed to cool for a few minutes. Infuse for three to four minutes.

Drinking suggestions: Drink without milk, alone or with light savory foods.

Supplier: Mariage Frères was established in Paris in 1854 and sells more than 400 different types of tea. The compant has a wonderful tea room where teas are brewed to perfection,

teas from around the world

Above: The Chinese frequently use mugs with a lid to preserve the heat of their tea.

tea

Classic Blend

Northern Tea Merchants
Crown House
193 Chatsworth Road
Chesterfield
Derbyshire S40 2BA
UK
Tel: (00 44) (0)1246 273611
or (00 44) (0)1246 232600
Fax: (00 44) (0)1246 555991

Over the years, individual companies have created favorite blends to suit different customers and different times of day. If breakfast blends are strong and rich, afternoon blends are much lighter and often include Chinese black leaf or the golden sparkling flavors of teas from Sri Lanka. They may be flavored with a little jasmine, bergamot or lemon.

In the past, royal names were often given to special blends but the use of the name of princes and princesses, dukes and duchesses is not permitted by those concerned today, although historical names, such as Queen Anne or Duke of Wellington, are still linked with some popular blends. Blends are much more likely today to have such names as Connoisseur blend, Boston Harbor Blend, London Blend, Classic Blend, After Dinner Tea, or even World Peace Blend.

There is nothing to stop tea drinkers creating their own blend. It is simply a matter of experimenting with different teas in different proportions until a pleasing mixture is discovered to suit the occasion and the drinker.

Northern Tea Merchant's Classic Blend is a mixture of African, Indian and Ceylon teas.

Characteristics: Small, quick brewing leaf that gives a bright-colored infusion that is full of strength and body.

Brewing hints: Infuse for two to three minutes in boiling water.

Drinking suggestions: Drink with milk as a breakfast or afternoon tea.

Supplier: Northern Tea Merchants' packaging includes a reproduction of a drawing of the crooked spire of Chesterfield cathedral. Built in 1234, it leans 8ft (2.5m) from the center.

tea

Darjeeling First Flush

Marco Polo Products Pte Ltd
79 Chitrakoot Building
230-A AJC Bose Road
Calcutta — 700 020
INDIA
Tel: (00 91) 33 247 1036
Fax: (00 91) 33 247 7508

Darjeeling is a small town that lies 6,000ft (1,800m) above sea level in the foothills of the Himalayas in the north east corner of India. Legend tells how a thunderbolt cast down to earth by Lord Indra — the king of heaven in Indian mythology — fell in Darjeeling. The Tibetan "dorje" means thunderbolt of Indra, and "ling" means place or land, so this is the land of Indra's thunderbolt.

The first tea gardens were established on the slopes of the mountains in the 1860s and today there are 86 estates producing 10,000-11,000 tons (10-11 million kilos) of tea every year. It is impossible to say exactly what it is that makes Darjeeling teas so distinct in flavor. The cool damp climate, the altitude, the amount of rain, the soil, the type of bush and the mountain air are all factors that contribute to its unique quality. The teas that are gathered in March, as the plants begin to shoot after the first sunshine of the early spring, give a flowery taste and aroma and an astringent flavor a little like that of green muscatel grapes. These teas are sought after by connoisseurs all around the world.

Characteristics: Large pieces of neatly twisted dark-brown leaf with lots of coppery and silvery-green pieces. The infusion is pale in color and astringent and flowery in taste.

Brewing hints: Brew in boiling water for two to three minutes.

Drinking suggestions: Drink without milk as an afternoon tea alone or with light foods.

Supplier: Goomtee Tea Garden, owned by Marco Polo Products Pte Ltd, was originally planted in 1899 and today produces some of the finest first and second flush Darjeelings.

tea

Darjeeling Second Flush

Upton Tea Imports
231 South Street
Hopkinton
MA 01748
USA
Fax: (001) 508 435 9955
e.mail: uptontea@tiac.net

The bushes that are cultivated in the Darjeeling district have been grown from both the Chinese hybrid of the tea plant and Assam variety. The Chinese-type plants can withstand quite cold conditions and therefore grow better at higher altitudes, but the Assam type bushes prefer heat and humidity and do well at lower elevations. The plants all stop growing during the colder winter months and start to push out new shoots in the spring. After the first flush has been gathered, the second flush or "summer teas" are picked in May and June and the succulent leaves give a liquor that is more mellow and fruity in taste than that of the first flush teas. Many people prefer the second flush for this reason.

Darjeeling accounts for only about 3% of India's tea production and the teas are in great demand from buyers in all the world's tea drinking countries. In the past, unscrupulous traders have mixed Darjeeling teas with teas from other regions and sold it as pure Darjeeling. Today, the Darjeeling logo of a picker holding a stem of one new bud and two leaves can be found on packets that contain only teas from this very special tea growing district. The details are for Singbulli Second Flush

Characteristics: An unusually bold leaf with the variegated colors of a very tippy tea. The infusion has an intense depth and concentration of flavor. Smooth and easy on the palate.

Brewing hints: Brew in boiling water for three to four minutes.

Drinking suggestions: Drink without milk. An excellent afternoon tea.

Supplier: Upton Tea Imports was founded in 1989 by Thomas Eck, a computer veteran and tea lover. He specializes in single estate teas.

Whittard
OF CHELSEA

DARJEELING
LEAF TEA
The champagne of teas

Brews .... ength 2

Darjeeling Blend

Bettys & Taylors of Harrogate
1 Parliament Street
Harrogate HG1 2QU
UK
Tel: (00 44) (0)1423 886055
Fax: (00 44) (0)1423 881083

As well as first and second flush teas, Darjeeling also produces very good teas through the monsoon period from mid-July to September and during the fall period in October and November. Monsoon teas have more color and a stronger flavor while the fall teas give a coppery-colored leaf and a more delicate infusion. Some of these are marketed as speciality single estate teas, but most go into Darjeeling blends which, by careful mixing and balancing of leaves from different seasons and different estates, should still have the lightness of flavor and slightly fruity character that are so typical of this area.

Many of the Darjeeling gardens have been replanted over the last few years with clonal bushes that have been propagated from carefully selected mother plants that produce well and are more resistant to disease.

Each garden has its own factory where most of the green leaf is still processed by the orthodox method of manufacture. The leaves are carefully handled with a skill that has been handed down through the generations but producers are constantly looking for new techniques and modern concepts that will improve their teas.

Characteristics: A broken leaf tea, selected from the highest gardens in the Himalayan foothills, that gives a mellow and aromatic infusion.

Brewing hints: Infuse in boiling water for four to five minutes.

Drinking suggestions: A refreshing afternoon blend, best drunk without milk.

Supplier: Taylors of Harrogate was founded in 1886 as a tea company but today sells a range of quality coffees as well as teas from around the world.

Above: Bettys and Taylors tea house in Harrogate, UK.

tea

Earl Grey

Twinings
216 Strand
London WC2R 1AP
UK
Tel: (00 44) (0)171 353 3511

The best-known stories about the origins of this bergamot-flavored tea tell how, in the days when Earl Grey was British Prime Minister (1830-1834), one of his diplomats on a mission in China saved the life of a mandarin and, by way of thanks, was given the recipe for the blend. It was then taken home and presented to Earl Grey who drank it as his preferred blend. It is impossible to know whether this is an accurate story or simply a marketing ploy to sell more of this extremely popular tea. It is true that the Chinese have traditionally used bergamot as one of the flavorings for their teas and it gives black or green leaf a refreshing citrus taste.

Each company that blends Earl Grey uses a different type of leaf and a different balance of flavoring. It can make quite a difference and too much bergamot will make the citrus flavor over-powering, whereas too little will not be strong enough. But, as with all teas, if the aroma, taste, and quality are to be preserved, it is important to store the tea in an air-tight container in a cool, dry place away from other strong smells.

Characteristics: Black leaf that gives a rich, red brew with a lightly citrus flavor.

Brewing hints: Infuse in boiling water for four to five minutes.

Drinking suggestions: Drink without milk at any time of the day. Particularly good with lemon flavored and creamy cakes and desserts.

Supplier: R Twining & Sons is the oldest of Britain's tea companies, dating back to 1706 when Thomas Twining opened Tom's Coffee House in the Strand just outside the city of London, and sold fine teas and coffees to the aristocracy and royal family.

English Breakfast

Grace Tea Company Ltd
50 West 17th Street
New York NY 10011
USA
Tel/Fax: (001) 212 255 2935

Most English and Scottish breakfast blends offer a strong, full-bodied flavor that complements rich breakfast foods such as bacon and eggs, smoked fish, ham, toast and marmalade, etc. The blends usually contain malty Assams, golden flavored Ceylons and strong dark Kenyan or other African teas, but each blending company will use an individual mix of teas that have been carefully selected by professional tasters to give a consistent taste.

The reason for the effectiveness of strong teas to wake us up in the morning is the gentle release of their caffeine content into the nervous system. The other chemicals in tea control the speed at which we absorb the caffeine and make it slower than when we drink coffee. After 15 to 20 minutes, tea's effects will be felt as refreshing and revitalizing, and less harsh than coffee's sudden burst of energy.

Keemun is thought by many to be one of the best traditional breakfast teas. It has a rich smoothness that is very palatable first thing in the morning and accompanies breakfast foods very successfully. This winey Keemun English Breakfast blend from Grace Teas is a prize winning best seller.

Characteristics: Congou-style leaf that gives a wine-like depth, body, and color.

Brewing hints: Infuse for four to five minutes in boiling water.

Drinking suggestions: Although best drunk without milk, some people may prefer to add just a little. Excellent for breakfast or as an accompaniment to afternoon tea.

Supplier: Grace Tea Company is a family business under the direction of Marguerite and Richard Sanders who formerly imported speciality foods into the US from China, Taiwan, and Hong Kong.

Flavored Teas

The Republic of Tea
8 Digital Drive
Suite 100
Novato CA 94949
USA
Tel: (001) 415 382 3400
Fax: (001) 415 382 3401

The Chinese tradition of flavoring leaf tea with flowers, fruits, herbs, and spices has been developed in different ways by different cultures. Some of China's teas are naturally perfumed by the flowers or trees that grow among the tea bushes — orchid flavored teas are a speciality from Zhejiang province.

In North Africa, green and black teas are flavored with mint, while in India, the leaves are boiled up with milk, sugar, cardamoms, and cloves. The best known and most popular of the classic flavored teas are Earl Grey (scented with oil of bergamot), rose, and jasmine, but today there is a wide range of flavors available which are extremely popular in Europe, Scandinavia, and the US. The concentrates and oils are almost all manufactured and supplied by two or three companies in Germany and the base is often a black leaf tea from China although more green flavored teas are beginning to appear on the market.

The Republic of Tea says of their vanilla almond tea "the smoothness of real Madagascar vanilla beans takes over the first sip of this tea, sweetening the cup. A nutty almond note follows, which send sit soaring into the realms of dessert."

Characteristics: Black leaf tea blended with vanilla pods and pieces of almond to give a sweet, soft infusion.

Brewing hints: Infuse in boiling water for four to five minutes.

Drinking suggestions: Drink without milk as a refreshing brew at any time of day or night.

Supplier: The Republic of Tea was launched in 1992 and sells an extensive range of rare and unusual black, green, oolong, and scented teas that are available in more than 1,500 stores across North America.

Above: The Republic of Tea makes a selection of flavored teas.

Formosa Oolong

Harney & Sons
Village Green
PO Box 638
Salisbury CT 06068
USA
Tel: (001) 860 435 5050
Fax: (001) 860 435 5044

Tea production started in Taiwan about 140 years ago when tea planters from China's Fujian province moved to the island of Formosa — as it was then called. They took with them tea plants and equipment and continued to produce the same type of oolong tea that they had manufactured in Fujian. As in China, after the leaves have been gathered, they are withered, spread out in baskets or on a large cloth in the sunlight, then they are rolled, oxidized, and dried. Sometimes the leaves are rolled tightly into large balls inside linen bags which are rolled by machine, then the leaves are separated by hand and fired to further reduce the moisture in the leaf. Eventually, the leaves turn to a coppery-brown color which give a delicate flavor.

Taiwan's tea growing areas are in the western central and northern parts of the island and the best teas are gathered from April through to October. One of the most famous of Formosa Oolongs is Tung Ting (Frozen Summit) which is made from leaves plucked on the highest mountain peak. The island also produces Lapsang Souchong and green tea.

Characteristics: Reddish-brown leaf that gives a pale amber liquor with a gentle aromatic flavor.

Brewing hints: Infuse in boiling water for five to seven minutes.

Drinking suggestions: Drink without milk. Excellent at any time of day and especially after a main meal.

Supplier: John Harney set up his tea company almost 30 years ago after running The White Hart Inn in Salisbury, Connecticut, for many years. His sons, Paul and Michael, now travel the world in search of the finest teas.

tea

Gunpowder

Torz & Macatonia Ltd
The Roastery
12 Blackwall Estate
Lanrick Road
London E14 0JP
UK
Tel: (00 44) (0)171 515 7770
Fax: (00 44) (0)171 515 7779

The reason for the name of this Chinese green tea is the fact that the little round balls look rather like lead shot. Each grey-green pellet is a whole leaf which unfurls and acquires a greener hue when infused in hot water. It is called by the Chinese "zhu cha" meaning pearl tea and was originally made in Zhejiang province which lies on China's east coast, but is today also made in other provinces in the same area.

Because of the ancient Chinese link between tea and Buddhist temples and monasteries where the plant was originally cultivated, many of the famous plantations are also tourist attractions and places of great beauty. The Chinese have a saying; "High mountains, pure water, good tea," and the best teas are grown high up among mists and clouds. The first crop is gathered in the spring from mid-April to mid-May. A second harvest is plucked in early summer and some regions pick a third, fall crop.

Gunpowder teas are made by first steaming the leaves to soften their surface, then they are rolled and fired.

Characteristics: Little grey-green balls give a clear, amber liquor, a sweet aroma, and a penetrating pungent taste.

Brewing hints: Brew in water that has boiled and been allowed to cool a little and infuse for three to four minutes.

Drinking suggestions: Drink without milk. Good with savory foods or as an after-dinner digestif.

Supplier: Jeremy Torz and Stephen Macatonia set up in business a few years ago to sell speciality coffees but now also offer a range of quality teas including greens, such as gunpowder and jasmine.

GUNPOWDER 125g

TORZ & MACATONIA FINE TEA MERCHANTS TEL 0181 500 2195
THIRZA HOUSE MANOR ROAD LAMBOURNE END ESSEX RM4 1NB

tea

Irish Breakfast

SpecialTeas
500 Summer Street
Suite 404
Stamford CT 06901
USA
Fax: (001) 203 975 4566
e.mail: service@specialteas.com

The Irish drink more tea than any other nation in the world and they like their tea strong and full of flavor. So Irish breakfast blends are generally even richer and blacker than English breakfast teas. Since the 1950s African teas, especially from Kenya and Malawi, have come to replace the more traditional Assams.

Today's breakfast blends tend to use CTC teas that are manufactured to create conveniently fast brewing small leaf. The general rule about brewing times for black teas is the smaller the leaf, the quicker it brews and vice versa. And the stronger the tea the higher the caffeine content and therefore the more noticeable the invigorating nature of the brew. For anyone who is careful about caffeine intake, the lighter Chinese black teas, such as Keemun and oolongs have a lower caffeine content, while green teas have the least. Decaffeinated teas are also available but tend to lack flavor and body, while green teas have the least caffeine.

Characteristics: A blend of China and Indian black teas from Assam and Nilgiri in the south of India, giving a robustness that has a smooth, slightly lemony flavor.

Brewing hints: Infuse for three to four minutes in boiling water.

Drinking suggestions: Best with milk as a very fine, strong breakfast tea.

Supplier: SpecialTeas offers a wide selection of single estate and blended teas from all over the world, fruit and herbal infusions, and tea accessories.

Jasmine

Peet's Coffee & Tea
PO Box 12509
Berkeley
CA 94712-9901
USA
Tel: (001) 510 594 2950
Fax: (001) 510 704 0311
e.mail: mailorder@peets.com

Ever since the Chinese started producing tea they have flavored the finished leaves with flowers, fruits, and spices. There was also a time when onions, peach leaves, salt, sugar, cinnamon, or cloves were added to the infusion once the tea had been brewed. All tea, whether green, oolong or black, absorbs other flavorings very easily and, simply by mixing blossoms in amongst the pieces of processed tea, a different final flavor is achieved. Traditional Chinese additions are magnolia, osmanthus, gardenia, bergamot, honeysuckle, orchid, and jasmine.

Jasmine flowers open at night, so the new blooms are gathered during the day and stored until they begin to open in the evening. Then they are either blended into the tea (usually green tea is the base) in a machine or piled next to heaps of tea so that the fragrance permeates across. The scenting process is carried out several times, with the more ordinary grades being scented twice or three times and the very best grades up to seven times. The blossoms that are mixed into the tea when it reaches the shops are added as a last stage just for appearance. The tea is often the first thing served in Chinese restaurants and is very refreshing.

Characteristics: Green pieces of twisted leaf with jasmine blossoms give a sweet, refreshing infusion with a wonderful perfume.

Brewing hints: Infuse for three minutes in water that has boiled and been allowed to cool.

Drinking suggestions: Drink without milk, alone or with light savory foods and desserts. Also excellent after a meal.

Supplier: When Peet's store first opened in 1966, teas were brewed by the cup for customers to sample. Today, the company markets a range of teas from the world's best known growing regions.

tea

Keemun

St James's Teas
Sir John Lyon House
Upper Thames Street
London EC4V 3PA
UK
Tel: (00 44) (0) 171 236 0611
Fax: (00 44) (0) 171 454 0006

The Chinese drink only white, green or oolong teas and the black teas which they produce are all manufactured for export. In the days of the 17th century, when China was shipping teas all around the world, merchants realized that their green leaf teas did not travel or keep well, but they discovered that if they dried, oxidized and fired the leaves, the black tea which resulted safeguarded their profits much better. Most tea drinking countries in those days drank both green and black teas but most, including Britain, gradually turned more and more to black.

Keemun is made in China's Anhui province where black tea production is thought to have started in the 1880s. The skill involved was learned from Fujian tea producers and, as the first factory found success, others also changed from making green tea so that today Anhui is famous for what is sometimes called the "burgundy of China black teas." It is a "congou" style tea, a name which comes from the word gongfu referring to the "disciplined skill" involved in its manufacture.

Characteristics: Thin, twisted strips of very black leaf that give a rich, brown infusion with a heady perfume and delicate flavor.

Brewing hints: Infuse in boiling water for five minutes.

Drinking suggestions: Drink without milk. Excellent with lightly spiced foods or after a main meal.

Supplier: St James's Teas has its offices in what was once the heart of the UK tea world in the city of London. They specialize in mail order and supply tea merchants all over the world.

Kenya

Stash Tea
9040 S W Burnham Street
Tigard
Oregon 97223-6199
USA
Tel: (001) 503 684 4424
Fax: (001) 503 624 9744

Tea production in Kenya started in 1903 but it did not become a viable commercial crop until the 1950s. The main tea areas are in the Kenya Highlands and most of the tea is grown by small-holder farmers who sell their green leaf to factories nearby. Because of steady temperatures and plenty of rainfall, the plants flush all year, although the best are harvested between late January and July. Almost all the teas are manufactured by the CTC method which gives tiny grainy pieces of leaf that brew quickly and give a richly colored, strong brew. These small leafed teas are ideal for use in tea bags and blending, and packing companies in both the US and the UK today import far more tea from Kenya and other African countries than they do from the traditional producers of India or Sri Lanka. In fact Britain buys roughly 50% of all tea imports from Kenya.

One estate, Marinyn, consistently produces high quality orthodox tea that instead of going into tea-bag or breakfast blends as most African teas do, is a excellent self-drinker and is particularly good with rich chocolate cakes or desserts.

Characteristics: Tippy leaf that gives a golden red liquor with a strong rich fruity flavor.

Brewing hints: Infuse for two to three minutes in boiling water.

Drinking suggestions: Best drunk with milk as an all day tea, and particularly good with rich tea-time foods.

Supplier: Stash Teas, founded in 1972, takes its name from the word used by the captains of tea clippers for their "private reserve" of the finest teas.

tea

Lapsang Souchong

Mark T Wendell
50 Beharrell St
PO Box 1312
W Concord MA 01742
USA
Tel: (001) 508 369 3709
Fax: (001) 508 369 7972

Lapsang Souchongs all come from China's Fujian province or from Taiwan. They are distinctive for their smoky, tarry flavor which is said to have been invented some time during the Qing Dynasty between 1644 and 1912. The legend tells how a unit of the Chinese army needed somewhere to sleep for the night and took over a tea factory. This obviously slowed down production of teas for the next day's market and when the leaves were not dry in time the next morning, the factory workers decided to light a fire of white pine to speed up the process. Apparently the smoked flavor was a great success and so the process was refined. The secrets of its manufacture are closely guarded by the Chinese and although visitors are allowed in the area where it is made, they are never permitted to go inside the actual factory. As far as we know, the smoking is carried out after the leaves have gone through the normal withering, pan-frying, rolling, oxidizing, and drying processes.

The word "souchong" refers to the variety of plant (that grows in the Wuyi Mountains of Fujian) which is used in the manufacture of these teas.

Characteristics: Black twisted shiny pieces of leaf that give a dark red liquor with a smoky aroma and taste.

Brewing hints: Brew in boiling water for four to five minutes.

Drinking suggestions: Drink without milk. Particularly good with smoked salmon and other smoked fish and meats.

Supplier: Mark T Wendell Importers dates back to 1852 when Mr. Wendell's uncle set up a company which traded with China and other producing countries. Today, the company is famous for its Hu-Kwa Lapsang.

Organic Tea

Ambootia™ Tea Estate
34a Metcalfe Street
Calcutta 700 013
INDIA
Tel: (00 91) 33 225 0015
or (00 91) 33 225 5771
Fax: (00 91) 33 225 9511
e.mail: ambootia.tea@smk.springtrpg.ems.vsnl.net.in

Organic teas are now widely available in the mail order catalogues of all the best companies, on the shelves of quality department stores, and in ordinary supermarkets.

Like a number of tea gardens around the world, Ambootia™ Tea Estate in Darjeeling has turned to organic tea manufacture and has been certified by the Institute of Market Ecology of Switzerland.

Ambootia™ has been producing teas since 1861 but has only recently been converted to organic farming methods. As on other organic estates, Ambootia's™ soil is treated with natural fertilizers such as compost and green manures, erosion is kept under control by planting soil cover plants and any pests are controlled by natural systems that use such insects as ladybugs instead of spraying chemicals onto the crops. There is also a concern for the welfare of the people who work the gardens and social harmony is as important as a harmony with nature.

Characteristics: Long, stylish, blackish-brown, twisted pieces with a purple hue and some green particles. Gives a brownish-red infusion and a smooth, sweet, mature flavor.

Brewing hints: Brew for three to four minutes in boiling water.

Drinking suggestions: Drink without milk at any time of the day.

Supplier: Ambootia™ Estate in India's north east state of Darjeeling produces black, green, oolong, and flavored organic teas. Its symbol is the ladybug that assists in the biodynamic method of farming.

Ambootia's™ packaging is as carefully prepared as its tea.

Rose Congou

Simpson & Vail Inc
PO Box 765
3 Quarry Road
Brookfield CT 06804
USA
Tel: (001) 203 775 0240
Fax: (001) 203 775 0462
e.mail: info@svtea.com

This delicately scented tea is made from a large leafed black tea blended with rose petals. Like Keemun, this is a "gongfu" tea that needs very careful handling, timing, and temperature control to reach the high standards demanded by graders and exporters. Teas are exported by private sale direct from producer to retailer in the consuming country, or through large provincial cooperatives that have offices in the main towns.

The names given to Chinese teas can be confusing. They can tell which province the tea is from (and the spelling and pronunciation for this can vary according to whether it is standard Chinese or dialect that is used); they can also give a specific village or town name; additionally, they can denote the method by which the tea has been manufactured, or the name may give a legend about the origins and mythical background to the tea. With all the possible Chinese forms for each word and the different phonetical transfer of each of those into English, terminology can become muddled.

Another rose scented tea that is widely available is Rose Pouchong which is made from a leaf that has been oxidized for a shorter time than oolong and then mixed with rose petals.

Characteristics: A clear, amber infusion with a sweet, fragrant taste.

Brewing hints: Infuse for five to seven minutes in boiling water.

Drinking suggestions: Drink without milk, alone as a refreshing afternoon or evening tea.

Supplier: Simpson & Vail was set up in 1904 in the port area of New York that was famous for its tea importers. Now located in Connecticut, the company sells a very wide range of teas, coffees, tea brewing and storing equipment, herbals, coffees, china wares, and food products.

Russian Caravan

Twinings
216 Strand
London WC2R 1AP
UK
Tel: (00 44) (0)171 353 3511

When China started exporting tea to Russia, supplies were carried from the tea growing areas to the trading post on the Russian border at Usk Kiahta. The Russians arrived with camels carrying furs from Moscow, the shipments of the different goods were exchanged and the tea was packed into cloth bags to be carried on the camels backs. As the camel caravan journeyed slowly back to the capital, campfires were lit each evening to cook food and keep the travelers warm. It is said that the smoke from the fires was absorbed by the tea and so created the now famous flavor of Russian Caravan blends.

Russia has been drinking tea since the end of the 17th century when a trade agreement was signed. Russian tea is brewed using boiling water from the elegant samovars that still take pride of place in many Russian homes. A strong concentrated infusion is brewed in a small pot which sits on the top of the traditional water heater to keep hot and when cups of tea are needed a little of the concentrate is poured into cups and topped up with water from a tap on the side of the samovar.

Characteristics: Black China leaf that gives a reddy-brown infusion with a slightly smoky flavor.

Brewing hints: Infuse in boiling water for three to four minutes.

Drinking suggestions: Drink black or with a little milk at any time of the day.

Supplier: R Twining & Sons is the oldest of Britain's tea companies, dating back to 1706 when Thomas Twining opened Tom's Coffee House in the Strand just outside the city of London, and sold fine teas and coffees to the aristocracy and royal family.

Sencha

The Tea House
15 Neal Street
London WC2H 9PU
UK
Tel: (00 44) (0)171 240 7539
Fax: (00 44) (0)171 835 4769

The Japanese traditionally drink green tea, and of the eight or nine different types manufactured, Sencha is the everyday brew.

Commercial tea production was established north of Kyoto in the 12th century AD and today, the main growing regions are in the southern part of the island and the western central area. The bushes are grown in long undulating waves that, for all but the very best grades, are plucked by machines. The leaves are immediately taken to the factory for steaming, rolling, drying, and sorting. The main varieties are dark green sweet-tasting Gyokuro, the best quality that is carefully picked by hand from bushes that are shaded from bright sunlight for three or four weeks before plucking; Tencha, a finely chopped high quality tea that is powdered in a special machine or traditional stone mill for the Japanese Tea Ceremony and whisked into boiled water with a special bamboo whisk; Sencha, the tea most commonly served; Bancha, a lower grade than Sencha; Houjicha, a roasted tea with a malty sweet flavor; and Genmaicha, made from Bancha leaves mixed with popped corn and toasted rice.

Never brew green teas with boiling water — it can make the tea bitter.

Characteristics: Flat green needles that give a clear, pale yellow liquor with a delicate, herby, pungent taste.

Brewing hints: Infuse for one to two minutes in water that has boiled and been allowed to cool for a few minutes.

Drinking suggestions: Drink without milk with light foods or alone at any time of day.

Supplier: The Tea House in London's Covent Garden opened in 1983 and today is well known as one of the capital's best sources of quality teas from China, India, Sri Lanka, and Japan. It sells a good range of flavored green teas.

Below: The Tea House offers many speciality teas, samples of which are displayed.

tea

Yunnan

Blue Willow Tea Company
911 E. Pike Street
Suite 204
Seattle WA 98122
USA
Tel: (001) 206 325 9889
Fax: (001) 206 328 0353

It is thought that commercial cultivation of tea began in China well before the birth of Christ and is today produced in 18 regions across the south of the country. About 80% of production is of green teas for the domestic market. Teas are usually marketed by the name of the region in which they are made.

The province of Yunnan, in the south west, is said to have been producing for more than 1,700 years. In the past farmers grew tea bushes as one of several crops and many still manufacture green teas for local consumption in their own kitchens. Most larger scale production of black teas for export is carried out by cooperatives, and while traditional manufacture was always done by hand, today factories are generally mechanized.

Yunnan is not very far from India's Assam tea growing district and it us therefore not surprising that Yunnan teas have a similar character to Assams. The plant grown in Yunnan is a broad leafed variety that pushes out fat buds and thick shoots and gives a spicy, peppery sort of flavor. Its stronger character means that it is the one China tea that drinks well with a little milk.

Characteristics: Black pieces of leaf with plenty of golden tips that give a rounded flavor with a hint of smokiness and a suggestion of oranges.

Brewing hints: Brew in boiling water for four to five minutes.

Drinking suggestions: Will take a little milk. Excellent for breakfast and with other meals.

Supplier: Blue Willow Teas sell a wide range of teas from all the major producing regions, including organic teas and herbals. They say that their Yunnan is their favorite breakfast tea.

tea

Acknowledgements

All photographs in this book, unless listed below, were taken by Simon Clay. The publisher would like to thank the following persons and organisations for supplying photography:

Page 5; Life File/Emma Lee
Page 7 (middle); Jeffrey Rabkin, DaCapo Images: DLWGraphics
Pages 7 (bottom), 9 (middle, bottom), 11 (top, bottom), 13 (top, bottom), 15 (top, bottom), 17 (top, bottom), 18; The Hulton Getty Picture Collection
Page 19; Corbis/Adam Wolfitt
Page 21 (top); Life File/Richard Powers
Page 21 (bottom); Life File/Jeremy Hoare
Pages 31 (bottom), 35 (bottom), 41; © 1998, 1997, Ambootia™ Tea Group (Photographer: James Prinz)
Page 44 - 45; Harney & Sons, Salisbury, CT
Page 65; Taylors of Harrogate

The publisher gratefully acknowledges the generosity of all the suppliers who provided tea samples for this book.

Every effort has been made to trace the ownership of all copyrighted material and to secure permission from copyright holders. In the event of any question arising as to the use of any material, we will be pleased to make necessary corrections in future printings.